Helping the Community

What Do FIREFIGHTERS Do?

Amy B. Rogers

PowerKiDS press
New York

Published in 2016 by The Rosen Publishing Group, Inc.
29 East 21st Street, New York, NY 10010

First Edition

Editor: Katie Kawa
Book Design: Katelyn Heinle

Photo Credits: Cover (firefighter), pp. 1, 21, 24 (helmet) Kris Timken/Blend Images/Getty Images; cover (hands) bymandesigns/Shutterstock.com; back cover Zffoto/Shutterstock.com; p. 5 Bob Peterson/UpperCut Images/Getty Images; p. 6 Johnny Habell/Shutterstock.com; p. 9 © iStockphoto.com/AlexSava; pp. 10, 24 (hose) Klesz/Shutterstock.com; pp. 13, 24 (ladder) © iStockphoto.com/christopherarndt; p. 14 potowizard/Shutterstock.com; p. 17 karelnoppe/Shutterstock.com; p. 18 Bplanet/Shutterstock.com; p. 22 bikeriderlondon/Shutterstock.com.

Library of Congress Cataloging-in-Publication Data

Rogers, Amy B.
What do firefighters do? / by Amy B. Rogers.
p. cm. — (Helping the community)
Includes index.
ISBN 978-1-4994-0626-9 (pbk.)
ISBN 978-1-4994-0627-6 (6 pack)
ISBN 978-1-4994-0628-3 (library binding)
1. Fire fighters — Juvenile literature. 2. Fire extinction — Juvenile literature. I. Rogers, Amy B. II. Title.
TH9148.R589 2016
628.9'25'092 —d23

Manufactured in the United States of America

CPSIA Compliance Information: Batch #WS15PK: For Further Information contact Rosen Publishing, New York, New York at 1-800-237-9932

CONTENTS

Firefighters put out fires.

Firefighters have to move quickly when there is a fire.

They go to fires in a fire truck.

FIRE DEPT.

Firefighters use **hoses** to put water on fires.

Firefighters use **ladders**, too. Ladders help them get to high places.

Firefighters help people get out of burning buildings.

Firefighters wear special clothes.
The clothes keep them safe.

They also wear boots.

Firefighters wear **helmets** to keep their head safe.

LIEUTENANT
2568

FIREFIGHTER
F.D.

Firefighters are brave!

WORDS TO KNOW

helmet

hose

ladder

INDEX

WEBSITES

Due to the changing nature of Internet links, PowerKids Press has developed an online list of websites related to the subject of this book. This site is updated regularly. Please use this link to access the list: www.powerkidslinks.com/htc/fire